First published in Great Britain in 1994
by William Heinemann Ltd
an imprint of Reed Children's Books
Michelin House, 81 Fulham Road, London SW3 6RB
and Auckland, Melbourne, Singapore and Toronto
Text copyright © 1994 Reed International Books Limited
Illustrations by Arkadia copyright © 1994 Reed International Books Limited
Based on the original television designs by Ivor Wood
copyright © 1994 Woodland Animations Ltd
ISBN 0 434 96709 2
A CIP catalogue record for this book is available at the British Library.
Printed in Great Britain by BPC Paulton Books

Postman Pat's

HEINEMANN · LONDON

"One, two, three,
Count with me."
Can you count with Postman Pat?

1 ⚫

2 ⚫⚫

3 ⚫⚫⚫

4 ⚫⚫⚫⚫

5 ⚫⚫⚫⚫⚫

6 ⚫⚫⚫⚫⚫⚫

7 ⚫⚫⚫⚫⚫⚫⚫

8 ⚫⚫⚫⚫⚫⚫⚫⚫

9 ⚫⚫⚫⚫⚫⚫⚫⚫⚫

10 ⚫⚫⚫⚫⚫⚫⚫⚫⚫⚫

1

one

Postman Pat has one cat called Jess.

two

There are two wheels on Miss Hubbard's bicycle.

3

three

Charlie Pringle has three books from the library.

4

four

There are four sheep crossing the road.

five

Pat buys five bananas from Sam Waldron's shop.

6

six

Pat has six parcels to deliver.

7

seven

There are seven chickens at Greendale Farm.

8

eight

Katy and Tom Pottage have eight marbles.

nine

Dorothy Thompson has nine tulips in her garden.

Mrs Goggins has ten letters for Pat to deliver.

Postman Pat has gone home to have tea with his family.

How many teapots can you see on the table?
How many cups and saucers?
How many sandwiches?

Jess is having a bowl of milk.
"Miaow," he says.

Goodnight.